NOTHING BETWEEN US

THE BERKELEY YEARS

*

A Novel in Prose Poems

*

WENDY BARKER

NOTHING BETWEEN US

THE BERKELEY YEARS

*

A Novel in Prose Poems

*

WENDY BARKER

—DEL SOL PRESS • WASHINGTON D. C.—

DEL SOL PRESS, WASHINGTON, D.C.

Paper ISBN: 978-1-934832-09-7

First Edition

Cover painting: Zachary Brown (b. 1982). *Straight On Till Morning,* 2008. Acrylic and mixed media on canvas, 18" x 24".

Cover & Interior Design by Ander Monson.

Publication by Del Sol Press/Web Del Sol Association, a not-for-profit corporation under section 501(c)(3) of the United States Internal Revenue Code.

CONTENTS

TEACHING *UNCLE TOM'S CHILDREN*

He was the only other honky in the room. But wasn't. Blond natural. Was his mother or his dad white or black? Kid played the best sax in town and only fourteen. Sax so sweet and cool the moon rose cream over the hills and stars broke the fog. He didn't talk much. Neither did I, that first Black Lit class any of us taught. I didn't know what to put on the board. Erased everything I'd written before, but the erasers were full of dust from the chalk. The blackboard turned powdery, a blur, clouded. We moved on through *Nigger, Black Boy, Native Son*. Not a kid caused trouble. Small sounds, fingers flipping the white pages of the paperbacks I collected and stacked in the corner cupboard after class. Slap of gum stretching in and out of a mouth, hard sole of a shoe on the floor, scraping the surface, an emery board. And the train, track barely a block away, the train running the whole length of the San Francisco Bay, cry moving ahead of it, toward us, that wail.

EUGUENE THOMPSON, THE HALL MONITOR

Old enough he'd sung "Old Man River" in most East Bay produc-
tions, but not so old he didn't still do it. I'd never seen a performance.
And wondered if he took his glasses off—so thick they ringed watery
circles round his eyes. Glaucoma, he told me, and he'd probably go
blind. He'd never seen his wife naked. Over thirty years and she always
had to be covered somewhere, wore a little flannel vest to bed, only
time he'd seen her breasts was when she nursed their first baby. They'd
even gone to the doctor because their sex had been so bad. Found out
her clitoris was a long way from where it's supposed to be, and that
explained it. But his little white lover over in Richmond knew what
he wanted, always opened her door to him without a stitch on, even
cooked him dinner like that. All the time he talked he'd be standing
in my classroom door. I'd never thought about anybody going to bed
with more than one person. You got picked for your role in life. You
sang it. You didn't cross town to try out for a different play.

HOME ROOM

A full period, fifty minutes, right before lunch. I had a traveling sched-
ule. Came all the way from the other wing, the third floor, and my fa-
vorite class. Those kids would even stick around after the bell, keep on
talking about *A Tale of Two Cities,* but I had four minutes to pack up
my books, lesson plans, my purse, and run down two flights of stairs
to make it on time. Thirty-eight kids in the typing room. The J's, all the
Johnsons and Joneses in the school. No Asians. Seven whites. The typ-
ing teacher Lillian Hillis didn't mind if I used the desk. I'd prop a book
next to the flowers she kept in a little jar. A long room. Dozens of Roy-
als and Underwoods covered up. Six of the Johnsons spent the period
leaning over the floor. I knew they were throwing dice. At least they
weren't fiddling with the typewriter keys, no little bell sounds of the
carriage return coming from their direction. On the board behind me
was the chart for finger positions. Right before lunch. Forty minutes.
The announcements took five. Attendance two or three. Handing out
forms maybe ten, but not every day. A window faced the courtyard.
One small tree grew out of the cement.

FOLKS

I didn't know what I'd been doing wrong in the Track 2 class. Till one of the counselors told me to stop saying *folks*. Not a friendly word, especially since the assassinations, Martin Luther King and Malcolm. Almost as bad as *coloreds, nigras.* Didn't even realize I'd been saying it—okay folks, time to get out your pencils. Thought of it as a neighborly word, an offering, sort of like a covered dish at a pot luck. A long way from my own folks in Phoenix. Family. During that first semester James Carmichael would stay after second period and help straighten the desks. Don't you worry Miss, they'll most of them be fine. Just take them a little time to get used to you.

One Friday around the middle of October, Calvin Jones cussed so much in class I led him out to the hall and leaned into his face: Look at me, look me in the eyes when I'm talking to you. At lunch the other teachers told me he was just being polite—you looked down, showed respect, never looked straight into the eyes of your teacher, especially your white teacher, especially your white woman teacher.

It was later in the year that James Carmichael joined the Black Muslims. New black slacks and tie, stiff white shirt. He'd been right, most everybody, even Calvin, had come around. But James had stopped smiling, his eyes gone somewhere else. He still turned in his work on time, still made B's. But there was nothing between us, never had been.

RELATIVE

My husband's Aunt Mary couldn't stop saying what a beautiful place we'd moved to. All year long, something blooming. And the houses, some excellent properties in the hills. Aunt Mary sold real estate in Tucson. What a climate on this coast, she said. And neither of us had to drive even ten minutes to our jobs. She'd taken Greg and me out for dinner at the Claremont. 180-degree view of the bay, all three bridges. Butter molded into rosebuds. Tomorrow we'd cross one of the bridges into San Francisco, maybe go the long way round to Marin, and take the Golden Gate back home. Maybe the fog would lift. She wanted to take me shopping, buy me new clothes. Start with Macy's, find me some things that would hold up. A good idea to stock up on high-quality, well-made, tailored clothes, discreet, tasteful, the kind that never went out of style. Some things were just classic.

REHEARSALS

I liked the high school's theater. Walls painted black, black curtains, no proscenium. I could sit up close, watch Greg as he led the orchestra in the pit, change seats whenever I wanted. The black walls worked really well for a play like *The Good Woman of Szechuan*. The drama teacher Paul did a Brecht play at least once a year, wanted the kids to experience politically and philosophically significant works. Musicals were harder to find. *West Side Story, The Fantasticks* were naturals for these kids, but shows like *Oklahoma!* or *Carousel* had been done to death, and besides, they were tearjerkers, crowd pleasers.

The back of Greg's neck. His hands, lifting to the violins, shifting over to the cellos. He'd bought a tux for the performances. This fall they were doing *Gypsy*. Little Nora Kaplan, a junior, her lilting mezzo, her reluctant strut down the ramp specially built to jut out into the house. Her precise and ladylike strip. Let me entertain you. Long black gloves, unbuttoning, inching down from Nora's slender upper arms, elbows, wrists, one finger at a time. A clarinet entering before the flutes. Paul's yells to everybody they'd have to redo the scene. Greg on his high stool, leaning over to the second violinist as they chuckled over something I couldn't hear. I'd grade papers, get some work done, and between scenes, a couple of the kids would keep me company, offer a sip of Pepsi.

The way they brushed my seat when I walked down the hall for a drink of water between classes. The little folds of the skirt, the red one, knit, so it kind of clung and then swept around me when I walked. I knew how I looked. Once one of the big black girls hollered at me as I was coming back from lunch, striding out between the cafeteria and my building, hollered out so anybody could hear, *why you wear your skirts so short, you already got a man.* So loud, it rang and rang even after the bell.

Seven classes a day. Two remedial. A hundred and sixty-three students. Four preparations, one of them Poetry of Pop Music. At home the guy who lived downstairs slammed open the door, clomped across the wood floor in his nailed boots at three a.m. before he'd play his Chinese funeral horn.

I was learning to serve in tennis, one of the PE teachers was helping. I'd bought a white tennis dress, its own panties sewn in. I could lift up, bend down as far as I needed, wherever the next ball came. When I got home, my husband was inside the headphones. Sometimes he came out to refill his glass, and sometimes he stayed inside for a long time.

SHOP TALK

We were having a drink at Harry's Bar across the street. Julie had been saying come on, how about Friday? After the halls and classrooms, the cafeteria, Harry's was like being inside an underwater cave. We were talking, whispering really, about the boys' PE teachers. Daniel was a sweetie, the football coach. Espinosa was married, with kids. Nice wife.

The tallest one? Ty? He means business. Julie's voice dropped further. I wouldn't encourage him unless—you mean business too. Our eyes held for a second. So many changes, we went on to say. So exciting with the new principal from Oakland, planning the alternative schools. So good to be starting with the mentally gifted, such great kids. Had to make sure we got the best faculty for them, that team had to be really strong. Another drink, Johnny Walker on the rocks, just a little water. Really, you know, I like what comes before the—actual real sex part best, do you? Julie tilted her head.

I guess I do too, I said, still not sure what to do with the little plastic straw they gave you. Finally I put it on the napkin that said *Harry's, a Berkeley Tradition.* Should I not talk to him at all?

That's up to you, Julie said. But be sure you know what you want. I fiddled with the peanuts, finally picked one out of the dish, sucked off the salt before I chewed, and asked Julie: What will happen to the teachers who don't want the alternative schools, don't want to team teach, even with all the federal money? Julie brought the rim of her glass close to her mouth and held it. She smiled, a big one. The teachers who get in our way? We'll run right over them.

Hilda had gone to check on the lentils. Phil sat in a half lotus on the wood floor. The first step, he said, was to stop talking so much. Listen to the silence. Even his sixth-period kids were mellowing, meditating ten minutes at least now in class. He'd moved out the desks. The kids had brought in old pillows and Hilda was sewing covers. Sitting at a desk was not a natural act. Besides, he'd all but quit giving writing assignments. They wasted resources, and he knew their grades anyway. English was not limited to the word. You had to stop talking to open the inner silences, like right this minute, he said, we should all stop talking, open ourselves. I started to close my eyes. But just then Hilda swung through the kitchen door and asked Phil if it was okay, sorry to interrupt, but could she put dinner on.

SUNDAY MORNING, GO FOR A DRIVE

Up the coast. Or down. Bring the binoculars. Get out of town. Breathe. Always hungry before we got where we were going, Stinson Beach, Bolinas, Point Reyes. Greg would want a big meal—two cheeseburgers, double order of fries, a full pitcher of Bud. I'd want a tuna sandwich, banana, orange juice. No matter how I'd try to focus the binos, no matter what rock I scrambled up on, I could never spot the bird I wanted to see up close. Feathers confused among branches and twigs. The wind off the water roughing my hair. And Greg's voice, breath smelling of tannic acid, saying hurry it up, time to go.

All the lights coming on, evening. A kitchen window, someone moving across the room. The trees darkening. The next house, kids around a table, a man pulling out a chair. I was jogging, trying to avoid the swollen places, cracked, in the squares of the sidewalk. Hills so steep up and down, my shins got a workout for a while and then my calves.

Greg had been talking about sod houses. Insulating with straw, you could even build partly underground. They did that in the Midwest. He'd begun ordering things from *The Whole Earth Catalog*. Maybe he'd make his own beer. On one page there was a picture of plaster molds made from four penises of different sizes and shapes lined up in a row. One was Jimi Hendrix's. They were numbered and named except for one that said, *A Friend.*

Three kids burst out from the bright opening of a front door, branches framing it. A porch light snapped on. Then four dark houses in a row. Then the gap, view of the flats, all the little lights, the red and white moving ones that were cars, and then the wide black opening of the water, the bay. But some of the places on land weren't lighted, and in the middle of the bay were buoys with beams flashing Hard to tell where the ground ended.

AFTER SCHOOL

The way the halls loosened, softened. You couldn't call what the coach-
es did walking. Even the metal lockers seemed to move. Those jogging
suits with zippers down their chests and straight up the sides of their
calves. Colors of candy, lollipops, suckers, lime, cherry, orange. Didn't
make a sound with their feet, the way they walked as if they were run-
ning but in slow motion, all the parts of their bodies moving together.
Mmmm. You new here? Where you from? What do you teach? Voices
like insides of M & M's. Halls cleared of kids, they moved through like
syrup through a snow cone.

Seven periods of trying to keep ninth-graders from shrieking, tear-
ing at each other. Somebody thrown into a locker, Pepsi and sudden
ice over the floor, slippery. All day I'd picked up trash, books, ragged
spiral papers.

The tallest coach would hang back from the others, stand at my door,
basketball nestled in the crook of his arm, talk direct as a shot clean
through the net. When the Home Ec teacher had a party where the air
hung thick and milky from the great dope somebody'd gotten out of
Nam, I went ahead and close-danced in the corner to Roberta Flack
until four. Seven periods a day, five days a week, telling the kids to
calm down, sit still, keep their hands to themselves, and I didn't move
his hand away when his fingers found my nipple and began to pull as
if it were soft, sweet taffy.

In one package you got the yarn, cloth for the pillow cover, and directions with a picture—a knight and his spear on a white horse clip-clopping along a green road lined with pink daisies toward a gray castle. I piled the papers that needed grading on the dining room table. French knots for the horse's eye and the flowers. Chain stitch for the leaves. I bought a half yard of linen, a book on American embroidery, made a sampler of stitches: stem, feather, star, cross, herringbone, running, and New England laid. Fewer weeks when the table was cleared. I began to work a remnant of burlap with thick wool. Stretched uneven petals zigzag across the weave. I'd been having the students do free-writing. Anything they wanted to say, the way they'd talk to a friend. Centers of flowers like eggs, spirals, like cocoons, leaves like wings. The flowers exploded in colors that shouldn't have mixed. Harder and harder to spot spelling errors, comma faults. The strands hurled across to each other. I stopped embroidering. Tired of prickings, the little stabs.

WORLD'S FINEST

I helped him carry in the cartons to the front hall closet. Just selling chocolate, Greg's orchestra kids could raise enough for their concert tour. I told him I'd find another place for the sheets and towels. He tossed the pillowcases on the hall floor before he lifted in the cartons. Couldn't keep them at the high school, they'd have been ripped off. They filled the space to the ceiling. White slick paper over silver foil, the high school's name on the outside, semisweet. He asked if I could go around the neighborhood when I came home from the ninth-grade campus and sell a few bars to the neighbors. He wouldn't have time, not with the extra rehearsals for the music festival coming up, not to mention his workshops out of town. I said I'd try. All that sweetness, wrapped up, inside.

SLOW DANCING

Ty didn't move much. At least his feet. But his legs, long thighs. And his cheek and mouth against my ear. His fingers holding mine to his chest. And that unmistakable cylinder rising against my belly. All for you, he whispered. Come to my place. Come tomorrow. He didn't bother stopping between songs. Most everybody gone when (and I couldn't believe I was doing this) I took my hand from his shoulder and reached down. For you, he said, again, so quiet. On the way home, fog billowed across the road, the white stripes, the dividing line.

DESSERT

A planning meeting at seven, I told Greg. I'd have to leave right after the dishes. No need to rush through dinner. After six years we were down to the basics, meat and a vegetable, maybe a salad. But no soup. Or pie.

I'd pressed the bell for the third time when Ty strolled up from the sidewalk. You like wine? I got us cream sherry. The man at the store said it'll be sweet. He keyed me in. The light from a single lamp. Two clear glasses.

We barely touched them. But it was sweet. And easy. Easy as the time when I was a little girl and my mother's friend said, go ahead, honey, it's just custard—milk, eggs, cream, they're all good for you.

Ten thirty by the time he turned the light back on. I said I'd come back, after school, Wednesday. He'd have a little snack for us, some cookies, or maybe ice cream. If I didn't mind eating on the couch. He didn't have a kitchen table.

REMEDIAL READING

The smallest classroom in the ninth-grade school. Yellow walls, and the ceiling seemed too high. Boxes lined up in bright colors on the tables, each a different level. This class for retards? This a toony class? The kids swaggered and straggled through the door, unwilling. To be seen here. Laminated cards, one at a time. Second-, third-grade skills for fourteen-year-olds. Mostly boys. I'd been assigned to help the reading teacher, her thick gray hair bunched and slipping along with hairpins and combs. Ruth organized field trips, took her own beat-up station wagon. Once she drove us up the coast to the great blue herons' nesting grounds. We walked up and up until we could look straight down into the tops of the big trees. She showed us how to spot the saucers of nests resting in the branches.

I never got the kids to move beyond a level or two. Nobody stayed on task. Once I was pronouncing vowels with Lester Sims, light-skinned, freckled, a skinny little dude. O: okra, Oakland, Coke. And o: butter, supper, dove. His eyes shone. He was standing beside me. Doves, he said. We can talk about birds? Sure, I said, and told him about the finches I was raising at home in as big a cage as I could afford. Man, why didn't you say you wanted us to talk about birds? and he was out the door. Before the bell rang for the next class he was back. I was putting cards away in their boxes, red tipped ones in the red box, brown in brown, folding the lids closed. You like pigeons? he grinned. I do, I do, I said. He unzipped his jacket. I don't know how many wings flapped out from him, ruffled my hair and fluttered all through that yellow room, a sound only feathers can make, as Lester told me every one of their names.

INTEGRATION

Almost lost in his mouth. He'd told me I didn't know how to kiss, I was trying too hard, and showed me, so our mouths ripened to plush opening peonies, ruffling, even a bit messy at the edges. More than a mother's mouth, nipple, these kisses. Shape to shape, unforming and reshaping, play of inner cheek and tongue. My consonants: so crisp, he said. Every one of my syllables clear, enunciated. But this now was a time for vowels, color, the fibrous textures of slow dipthongs, blurred edges letting i's blend into u's, long e's open into ah, o, oh, oh, oh.

ON THE BAY

It was the art teacher Norm who had the doctor friend who was leasing the twenty-seven-foot sailboat we took out onto the bay that Saturday before Margie the history teacher's party and we smoked dope all day on the water. There for a while we drifted out beyond the Golden Gate into the open sea before we knew what we were doing so it took about three hours just to get back under the bridge, everybody laughing except the one guy who'd had the six sailing lessons so he knew what was maybe about to happen. Norm was getting it on with Nini on the foam mattress under the prow and everybody else was sopping from the spray that was everywhere over us. That whole day no fog at all, even after we docked back at the Marina and stopped at the Safeway to pick up some Cribari red for the party where Margie had put out candles on the tables, all sizes and shapes burning down puddles of different colors of hot wax around their flames like the lights of the city we'd just spent the whole day sailing past, turned on.

HAIR

Not yet thirty and he was already bald but just on top. So his caramel-colored head rose over him, soft and glistening. But plenty of hair around the rest of his head, nappy, close. Mine was short, a pixie cut. Not even a few fringes drifting below my collar, or across my pierced ears. We'd done it in the kitchen, an ice cube behind each ear lobe. And my sister was right, it didn't hurt. So far I hadn't decided what kind of earrings to buy, so I stayed with the small gold studs, 24 karat.

The first time I'd gone to his second floor apartment—he'd been asking me for months—he said it was like a cherry. I hadn't known I could come on my own, before he did. He kept going and going, over me, he was staring out the window above the bed—later he explained he had to keep his mind off it or he'd finish too fast—and asked me, said, you haven't come yet, go ahead. When he turned on the light there were little black coils of hair all over the sheets. It wasn't long after that I decided to let mine grow, see what it did by itself.

SWORD

When I started weaving, Ruth gave me one. Funny to call it a sword. Hand-rubbed, dark grain of the wood smooth as a camellia leaf. So beautiful I could just hold it. But I learned how to separate the warp threads with the silky tip—lifting one thread up, keeping the next one down, up, down, again and again, all across the vertical strands. To turn the sword so it held the top threads out from the rest, make space to let the weft threads through. It worked as a comb, or beater, too, another funny word for working with so many kinds of softness, pushing the thread you've pulled across the loom's width down into the forming cloth. Strange how the sword parted the threads away from each other, lifted them and then pressed them down, firm, together. Soft thuds of wool on wool, and after a while, regular as your heartbeat.

FREED UP

He said I had nice ones, even though I'd always thought they were so little, but why did I bind them up? One day I left my bra in the drawer. All day could feel the feel of them. Couldn't forget they were there. Felt good just leaning down to throw a wad of paper in the trash. And standing up, nipples like third and fourth eyes, looking straight out at whoever was coming toward me in the long hall. Looking clear inside. Into secrets, hiding places. Until they were out for good, out of the muffled fiber-filled shells, elastic tightenings, hard-wire frames. Like bare green leaves unfolding in April, swelling as they opened. Leisurely, soft, brushing into a hand.

One of the counselors offered to teach me. Disaster to let my husband coach me on anything having to do with driving. If I could shift for myself, I'd have more control. After a while I practiced alone in a parking lot. Neutral, first, second. The timing with the clutch. And then, slowly, on the side streets off Marin. I kept away from the hills. But no matter how gradually I raised my left foot, the car always died at a stop sign. The honking behind me. I'd get so nervous I'd just stall and stall. When after a few weeks I'd managed okay on San Pablo, Shattuck, and even down University, I decided to try the freeway. At the entrance onto the Nimitz I could see across into the wetlands of the bay, a great blue heron along with the usual gulls. A car right behind me. Riding me, flashing its lights. Refused to pass. I let the clutch out, shifted, floored it, and eased over to the far left lane.

EGGPLANT

I'd never heard of it. A plant like an egg? Hilda's casserole at Ellie's party, mixed up with tomatoes and onions and olives. The eggplant didn't have much color, but it tasted good. Ellie said the French called it *aubergine*. A pretty word, sounded like jewelry, something shiny, an expensive watch—Longines. I couldn't find any at the Coop. Finally I asked the guy spraying radishes. Sure, right here, he said, and pointed to a pile of purple globes next to the carrots. But how could those pale cubes in Hilda's dish come from one of these? Oh yeah, he said, they're good, these are the kind called Black Beauty, they grow right here in California. He helped me choose a firm one with no bruises. It shimmered in my grocery cart, dark as midnight, purple as a royal orb. He said he couldn't tell me how to cook it, but he'd heard that in Turkey, there were over a thousand recipes. I didn't know even one.

TEACHERS' LOUNGE

Ken always sat in the pink high-backed chair. He'd started selling real estate on the side, just residential, he didn't want to get into apartment buildings, not with all the riffraff moving in these days. The whole place had changed so much he felt he was living on Mars. The trash on the streets now, and he meant human. Why the hair. He wanted me to know, because, he said, he could tell I was a nice person, not one of these wandering bums the school district was hiring, and he wanted me to understand this city had been the Athens of the West until the hippies started running it. Even just a couple of years ago the kids had manners. He thumped his pipe into the ashtray already filled with butts, cellophane strips from cigarette packs, paper clips and razor blades for correcting dittos.

I should have been grading papers. Or preparing. Compound sentences. Conjunctions. And, but, or. I was pouring water over a two-day-old tea bag when Ardis Baine the Latin teacher walked in, black eyes snapping, and slid her ditto master into the machine. Ardis had three degrees from Howard University. She glanced into my cup. What on earth are you drinking, honey, she said. After she left with the fresh damp stack of purplish paper in her hands, the room turned silent. My tea tasted like polluted water. The next day I brought in a jar of instant coffee. Made it strong and drank it black. That was before I stopped coming to the lounge at all, unless I had to use the machine to run something off.

SLIPPING IN

The first time I'd left Ty's place late, really late, the streets black-wet, quiet. Straight through a red light at Shattuck. Had to have my phrasing down pat, rehearsed—the meeting ran over, I couldn't leave, too racially sensitive, and Julie talked me into going out after. Even as I unlocked the front door I heard the snoring. Shoes and socks, tapes and LP's, the headphones, orchestra scores over the living room rug, the empty green gallon jug on its side. Dishes on the kitchen counters, the stove. Greg still dressed lying in bed, belt unbuckled, pants unzipped, wine glass on the floor. An orchestra, I told him the next morning, of snores—triple forte. But he only wanted to talk about the new score. After last night he was ready to put it into rehearsal. He showed me the conducting pattern he'd worked out, his arms driving tracks through the air. I was trying to get dressed, had to leave for school in ten minutes. Oh, he said, I forgot, how was your meeting? Okay, I said, okay, buttoning my blouse. Good, he said, but tonight I want to take you measure by measure through the whole score. Show you where the oboe slips in, before the violins take over from the cellos and bassoons. How the crescendos begin to build.

Ty had to explain what it meant when he told me, I got a nose job behind you. They said it back in Georgia—you couldn't stop thinking about somebody, you followed them around, you'd fallen for them, you were hooked. And he couldn't believe it, what with all that new pussy at school, all the new teachers. The Swedish one with the accent, her thick white-blond hair piled up on top of her head, stiff white blouses and high-neck collars, lace, maybe, but underneath, those great big soft boobs. And the German one—kind of like Marilyn Monroe but fatter, nice sloppy behind, and laughing, real friendly. And he still liked to check out the little sister from Kansas, the math teacher Roberta Gibson, those legs—sweet as cinnamon, those huge black eyes, close little natural.

Last year after school he'd always be going over to Ortman's for a double scoop, maybe triple. They kept getting in more and more new flavors, some of them better than Chocolate Mint Chip. Maple Swirl was a good one. Chocolate Marshmallow. And the kind they got in last June just before school was out, Coconut Almond Peach.

But this was different, he said. He was rubbing his nose into my neck. He'd brought the donuts into bed the way he did now when I stayed all night if Greg was out of town. Sunday morning, he'd get two of each: jelly, chocolate, and plain glazed. He was playing my nipples between his fingers, pulling them. Only woman who could take all of him, he said. And the way we talked. About anything, anytime, nighttime, daytime, like straight up noon when he'd bring his sandwich into my classroom and tell me about the morning, about still trying to teach that math genius kid named Gerald how to do setups, how to cut through the others and aim at that one place where you really wanted it, and score.

HALF AND HALF

I'd eaten less and less, no carbohydrates, mainly protein, hard-boiled eggs. At first I thought the school I'd been assigned to was ninety percent black. Naturals swirled black halos around me till even at home at night I thought I would disappear. By Halloween I knew it was more like half and half. That was around the time I heard the whispering outside my classroom door after everyone else had gone home, felt afraid as I had during the riots in South Side Chicago. The whisperings grew louder, what they would do to me. I stood up from my desk and walked right past them and down the hall to the principal's office before I started to cry.

All this was before Ty was there. Nobody knew, and we made sure we kept it that way, but I could think about him all day and at night, about the way his darkness slid right into me, how he filled me with himself until I felt I'd split open.

One Saturday night when I didn't go home, I stared for a long time at his one poster hanging on the wall. A little black boy dressed in white and sitting in a white chair in a room with white walls, white ceiling, and a white floor. Sometime in the night I started to shiver, cold without a nightgown. I was half asleep when he went to the closet, pulled down a brown wool blanket. From his mother, he said, when he left Georgia to play for Colorado. And he'd needed all the warm blankets he could get in Boulder, those high white mountains. He made sure I was covered up before he lay down again next to me. Sweet smell of his hair. In the morning I didn't want to leave. He brought the donuts into bed, the kind with the soft cream filling. That was when he told me where the scars on his shoulders came from. If you ever have a son, he said, don't let him play football. You can get torn up, bad, before your time.

CLAY

Some lunch hours Karen sat on top of my desk in her Levi's and tie-dye, swinging her legs while she bit into a ripe avocado. Solid vitamins, she told me as she swallowed. I'd be eating a ham sandwich. Salt, she said, too much. Meat. Her father taught philosophy at Cal, her mother did clay. When we had Arts Day for the Mentally Gifted, Karen brought two buckets. I got my hands down in it. Karen said, don't waste your time, whatever you make, there's no place we can dry it, there's no kiln. I mushed in and down till my hands were wet to the bone, and cold. Why don't you ever go up to the Avenue, march with us? Karen would ask. The sixth-period remedial kids were finally coming to school, most days. Hated hippies, wouldn't listen to any white woman who wasn't tidy-looking. I kept squeezing the clay, arms brown to the elbow, a second skin, thickening. I wasn't thinking of what could be made with the stuff.

MACRAMÉ

I never got into it. Too many knots. Rope or string, mostly white, or that pale yellowy color, twisted in on itself, maybe a few beads. All that work just to hold a house plant off the floor. I was weaving. Different yarns. Crinkly silk like hair from an unraveled braid. Silver. A fat wool, furry, the shade of lichen under a pine. And blue, a deep teal, turquoise, the way you remember an inland high sky in winter. Purple, fuchsia, orange, sunsets. Dawn. Sometimes I thought of the students I liked while I worked. Frances, her low voice, her cello. Jennifer's little giggles. Charles, his wide smile, giant Afro. Andrew, trying to get me to read *Dune*. The warp strands sturdy, brown. Backstrap loom tied to the window latch. I pushed the weft threads down, a soft thud. Over and under. One color showing more now, another the next time. I gathered eucalyptus bells that fell under the tall trees in the hills. Clean-smelling, a good medicine. I liked working the dark seeds into the pattern. I wanted to make something big, fill a space, soften a wall.

"HEY, MR. TAMBOURINE MAN"

The gravel of Dylan's voice rising from the floor below, *play a song for me*. Cold morning, the fog. I didn't want to grade papers. Didn't want to read. At least I had Ellie's party to look forward to that night. I'd wear the new striped dress I'd bought last weekend at Julie's parents' store, and the big dangling metal earrings from the Renaissance Fair. Greg wasn't going—didn't like Ellie's parties. The record downstairs wasn't all that loud, but already I was tired of Dylan's whine. Sometimes I wished he'd just open up the back of his throat. There it was, though, my favorite part, *dance beneath the diamond sky with one hand waving free.* I hadn't slept well, not much the last week or so. Somebody in the park had been playing a flute all night. Those pure high sounds piercing the air, over and over. Clear breath. Like a wide-open moon swimming through fog, full, into focus.

TENNIS

Ty didn't learn to play in Georgia. Not till he got to Colorado, the second year of his scholarship. One of the rich white girls took him out on the court. Little balls the color of vanilla ice cream, the new ones fuzzy as those soft bears the sorority girls kept on their day beds. Sound of the strings against the ball—after the first whack, one long vibration. Kind of like a Charlie Parker riff, he was saying. Or a cool trumpet. Miles, Miles Davis. Your turn, my turn, now you take it. Not like football, everybody coming at you. And those old white men pawing you at the half, give it to them boy, keep it up, doing great. Pawing you. All that dust, smoke, hollering. A tennis court's clean. Grass, clay, even cement, they're clean. You got your side to yourself. Doubles, only you and your partner. You got room to pull way up and way back to serve. That little ball just moves on out from your racket like a guitar singing a song—you hear this one? Now sing it back to me.

MAKING A BED

He liked the way I did it, asked me to show him. Not that he hadn't been doing fine himself. But my corners stayed. Think of geometry, I said. A sheet's just a big square, all the threads are straight lines intersecting at right angles, so start with them lined up on the mattress. Even. Flat. My hands slid across the surface of the bed. I slowed, leaned down to make the triangular fold at the corner. Ty bent down too, and the rest of the clean sheets, pillow cases, stayed on the chair, along with the blanket, the spread, and the crocheted afghan with orange nubs rising up like little buds, or stars—the browns and tans, blues and whites all curled into each other.

ALARM

I never got used to it. No warning, and it wouldn't let up, not like a shout, or a car backfiring, or gunshot. The tide of teachers and kids to the double glass doors, the gray light at the end of the locker-lined hall. Not every day, more like eight, ten times a month, some weeks worse than others. The questions. Fire drill? Another bomb? A real fire? Everybody trying to find their friends in the crowd of naturals, the typing teacher's tidy curls, Shirley Jensen's fly-away pony tail, Phil Friedman's brown waves to his shoulders, and the white girls' hair floating around them like scarves. Buffalo sandals, boots, Adidas, moccasins, clogs. At the doors, no way at first to move through.

As soon as I could I'd spot Ty. On the other side of the cement court-yard, he'd be cradling a basketball and joking with the boys around him. I knew exactly what he'd be saying: Stay cool now my man, stay cool. And he'd catch my eye, hold it so I'd stay calm, be able to talk to the kids around me, distract them. It could take an hour. The specula-tions. His eyes touched me every once in a while, but not so anybody'd notice. At opposite ends of the grounds behind the ninth-grade school, we stood so we never lost sight of each other, until the all-clear bell, when we crowded back into our separate buildings, and carried on.

GRANOLA

Ruth brought some in a cellophane bag. All natural, she said, good things in it. I needed to be fattened up. She knew I'd been drinking too much coffee since I'd bought the Melita pot with the filter. This stuff was brand new at the Coop. Raisins, dates, oats, almonds, I could snack on it, didn't even need milk, although that's what it was of course, cereal. I needed to feed myself better. Not to hurt my feelings, but did I know some of those bad-mannered kids called me Twiggy? She had to go now, get back to her husband who'd be wanting his supper, and then she had worksheets to grade tonight. A shame my husband was so busy, gone so much. I should come to dinner some-time. The fringe of her shawl brushed the wall by the front door. Her necklaces were made of wooden beads and seed pods. Every summer she went to Oaxaca. They wove every color you could imagine into their cloth, Ruth said. The new cereal wasn't like Cheerios. The closer I looked, the more ingredients I could see, even sesame seeds, tiny little ovals of white.

ADVANCED TECHNIQUES

Different ways of wrapping the warp. You could pull a few threads together, tie them, make little bundles. At our new alternative school teachers' meetings at lunch time, the twelve of us were dividing into groups. First into twos. After we'd decided what bird each of us wanted to be, we joined another pair. Then we all four drew our birds, showed them, and next we'd think of what character in a novel we were. Weaving I did alone, at home. I liked the bundles, bringing the threads so close they almost seemed like one. At lunch Fred said I always made him think of Catherine in *Wuthering Heights*. How she poured tea in the drawing room but her real self was racing the moors, calling for Heathcliff. I hadn't read it since high school. We didn't use that novel, even with the gifted students. I finished the tapestry with the bundles. Got an idea for the next one. The entire warp pulled into clusters, each one wrapped so long, so close, the entire fabric would open.

Luminous was the word he used. Repeated it. Yeah, he said, that's it, that's what you are. *Luminousness.* Each syllable a slow mouthful. *Luminescence.* His tongue and lips made full contact with every consonant, as if he were walking deliberately through a dark, vacant room, turning on all the lamps. But I never told him how even before he opened the door to my classroom, I would know. A quiet grew behind the clanging of lockers, the hollered motherfuckers. A soft silence that had nothing to do with speechlessness. The volume just turned itself down. Even in the middle of the hall's screeching at second lunch (*where you think you be walking to, honky bitch*) he brought with him a thick-carpeted room of sleek and steady upholstery, padded back and arms of a good chair. No fear of a lamp's being toppled, or the cord yanked.

NOTE CARDS

Stacks of them all across the bed. Where a fold of the blanket made a little hill, they slipped like shallow steps dropping down a slope. White with faint blue lines, 3 x 5. Ty's penciled writing. A big paper coming up for his graduate class, "Motor Skills in the Secondary Schools." One whole pile of cards on approaching the serve. Most people didn't understand—a good serve begins a long time before the racket and ball ever meet. The backswing. Preparation. You have to let the racket drop completely down your back before you bring it up over yourself and forward. Supposed to write it like a chapter in a textbook for teachers. Make it easy to understand. Hey, here's a good quote in this book, see, this lady, she teaches at UCLA, she's talking about building confidence in kids, says to divide all the skills into little parts. You let the kids get real good at one thing before you show them how to move on to the next. Yeah. I think I know what to do. The stance. The grip. See how you helped me already. His head turned to mine, that sideways smile. Let's get this mess off the bed.

SWEET

You know those cups you had growing up, he said, those paper cups with the wooden spoon that was sort of rough on your tongue. Half vanilla, other half orange sherbert. The Home Ec teacher had just told him about vanilla ice cream, how the taste of it came from a skinny brown bean. Funny, he said, you never thought about something like that, where the taste came from. And funny how I made him think of that kind of ice cream. All sweaty and out of breath from running bases as a kid, and some nice church ladies off to the side of home plate handing them out to everybody on the team. Take your time dipping into that stuff, nice and cold—good in your mouth. Some kids ate all of one kind first, saved the vanilla or the orange for last. Not him. He took some of each, every mouthful. Orange and white. When he pulled off the lid there they'd be, shaped kind of like those black and white designs they sold in the hippie stores, those Chinese things, black dot in the white part, white dot in the black. Sometimes when he'd peel an orange, the white fibers stuck to the fruit. He'd eat them too, had heard those stringy things were good for you. And he sure did love that new nightgown of mine, color of peaches, a little bit of lace, just like cream.

COURT

He liked our walks in the hills, especially afterward, when we'd dressed again, brushed the leaves and dirt off our clothes. At first he hadn't understood what my sport was, most people had at least one, volley-ball, softball, tennis. Sometimes he'd lead, sometimes I would. Once when we drove down the coast we climbed up over the road and up an embankment, slipping together in the mud, laughing, holding on to each other. Little pebbles, bits of roots. That night in the motel I said *look,* and he did. In the mirrors on the sliding closet doors like the two halves of a tennis court, net down, there we were. Stretched out across the whole length, his legs around my light ones, my arms over his back. Layers of us. Little movements. My hair, his neck. Leaves brushing. Murmurs, currents. When we'd climbed to the top of the embankment, we had to get our breath. The whole Pacific spread out.

SAX

Cool slow riff, under, over, around and around one central note that took a long time to find. The sheets ruffled across the bed and down, spread like a fan, a loose shawl. Wet spot dry now. Sprawled pages of the paper. Fog breezing into the window over the bed. His arms. Warm. As if I were wrapped in my own little girlhood, cradled for Vespers in my granddad's boat, oars shipped, stilled in the shallows of the evening lake as the singing began on shore, *carry me home, coming for to carry me*. All the notes of those voices. Ripples of the water, colors of pearl in the darkening, boat rocking. The wide water. Then back across, oars dripping, across the lake to sleep, in the long quiet of the night. Until waked by a cry coming from the center of silence, loon call, tremolo rising across the brush-tops of the pines in the blackness. Joined, by another, and another, by another.

CROSS WEAVE

Taffeta, for example. Our instructor Liz was explaining at the Wednesday night adult extension class. Warp and woof threads of two different colors. Plain weave, equally spaced. Both sides of the fabric identical. Usually contrasting colors, say for instance, burgundy, navy blue. From one direction you'd see more of one color. Turn a little, you saw more of the other. And the moment the cloth moved, whether gathered, folded, swinging out from you if you wore it—or even just rumpled, the colors shifted. Liz handed out samples. I shook mine, gently, watched it shimmer. The cloth turned fluid. Waves of shades, changing. It was a green, a blue green, iridescent. Mesmerizing, like the ocean. For a moment I could float in it, almost dive right in, and at the same time, never leave the air.

COUPLE

I didn't know why he said he'd never get married. He just said never. I
believed him. One weekend we drove up to Marin. Poked into shops,
and I bought a candle. Everybody strolling, families, couples, mostly
white. First time we'd done anything right out in public. But nobody
stared.

I couldn't imagine not being married to somebody. The every-morn-
ingness. The regular breathing beside you through the night. The
shoes lined up, left beside right, heels, flats, tennies, boots, wing tips,
sandals. Pairs. The same cups filled, sipped from, washed, put away
with the chips facing the back of the cupboard.

Ty licked his double scoop till the ice cream lay flat in the cone, and
then dug in with his teeth. I nibbled mine around the edges. He'd fin-
ished his cone, a little bit of his tongue slid over his upper lip. Good,
he said again. I was going to spend the night. He'd picked up eggs and
English muffins, didn't I like those, and the kind of coffee I drank now.
Sunday morning, Greg away on a concert tour, I could stay as long as
I liked.

CHOPSTICKS

We walked for blocks before we decided where to go inside to eat. Past plucked chickens and ducks, cucumbers, postcards, pale jade. Neither of us knew quite what to order. But we knew to ask for chopsticks. More fun that way, without the metallic scrape of the fork, the hard grate of a knife. Two slim prongs. Light wood. Each moving toward the other, each coming from another direction to grasp the same kernel, pod, grain, cube, sliver of carrot, ginger. We'd never been here before. Never to Chinatown together, even to San Francisco. Summertime. We had our sweaters with us. Took a long time to finish. I've had better, he said, but he ate everything I didn't have room for. Before we got back onto the Bay Bridge, we stopped for ice cream. I asked for lemon custard and coconut almond. His was rocky road and chocolate mint chip. We each licked and nibbled at our own cones, and then held them out so the other could taste, held them steadily, carefully, so none of the sweetness would topple over, fall.

He couldn't wait to show me. Now that Joanie his old girl friend had quit teaching in the Mission and was flying for American, she could bring them back from Frankfurt, Munich, places like that. New kind of knit material. Soft, stretchy, and not just white. Colors. Blue, and gold, and red, bright red like those flowers the stores put out at Christmastime. All the coaches wanted one. He was keeping the black and tan for himself. Only had to sell two more and he'd break even. After that, pure profit.

He didn't know why his main man Arthur Ashe only wore those boring old Munsingwear waffle knit white shirts with the little black penguin. Those wings sort of half down and half up like he was standing still all polite while somebody's saying, little bird, no way you can fly. Like he wouldn't know how to hold a racket if somebody handed him a brand new stainless steel Wilson. Like still hanging on to that old wood. Those little penguins—their days are past. Pretty soon there'll only be color, both sides of the net.

BREATH

Ellie was telling me over our tuna sandwiches in the teachers' cafeteria how to make a soufflé. The secret was in the egg whites, you had to whip as much air into them as you could. The word *soufflé* was like the French word for breath: *souffle*. I'd never made a soufflé, but *souffle* sounded like "poof," a little bit of breath, a soft blow on a fluffy dandelion seed head, all the tiny arrows flying off. Like picking petals from a daisy. *He loves me, he loves me not.* Ellie began describing her date for Friday night. He had nice hands and eyes, she whispered, and she wanted to touch him. They'd gone to a couple of movies, that was all so far. School had started again. I was tired of talking. Was picturing a soufflé rising in the oven. Wondered how you'd serve it onto your plate so it wouldn't collapse.

AUDIO VISUAL

One of the boys would help if the film broke. Some of them even knew how to fix the oldest projector, the one that sputtered and cluttered and moaned to a stop in the middle of the story. Like when Ulysses had himself bound up, so he could sail past the sirens, or when he was barely making it through between Scylla and Charybdis. A couple of the girls would stay and talk over their sandwiches at lunchtime about Mr. Taylor who always asked for help in the auditorium's projection booth whenever they showed movies for all the history classes at once. He'd accidentally brush against them in the dark, then take his time feeling them up. They laughed about it. Everybody thought he was pretty cute. The administrators had their eye on him to get his credential, be a principal in a year or two. Movie days were a relief. The sound drowned out the traffic on University Avenue, and even late in the afternoon, with the blinds down the pimps didn't bother to hassle their girls through the windows, hollering in, *Inetta, you get your black ass out on this street, Yvonne, you hear me girl.* Even with the volume turned up high, the sound track distorted, everything seemed just that much quieter.

CLASSICAL

Seventh period Track 3, the unit on myth. I started with Zeus, the big daddy, king of the gods. He liked to buzz on down to earth and dress up like a swan or a white bull, and kind of get involved, play around on earth. Like with Io, I said, or Leda, and every time, his wife Queen Hera got angry at those girls and sometimes even their children had to pay. I'd never seen them so wide awake after lunch. Mouths stopped sucking on Jujubes, stopped mid-chew. They just listened. Nobody fidgeted, scuffed the floor. I know what you talking about, blurted out Loretta. I gotta uncle just like him, got his hands busy over everybody, first my sister, then this Thanksgiving he mess with me. And my auntie, she don't do nothing. But she be mad. Christmas Day, she don't give me one present. And that old man, he won't show his face.

The way the dark rectangle shot up—slid—graphite slick, towering. Opaque. The Track 1 boys told me to read the book. Just one thing different, and everything changed. After the first time two of the pimps climbed through my windows to get their girls working the street by four, I never walked through my classroom door in the morning the same. Candy wrappers, dandelions, on the grass outside. And in the spring, the way the tanks snaked along University Avenue right outside my windows—every day a metal river, sludge flowing up the street my class looked out on—when Reagan called in the National Guard. Only the white students cared about People's Park. I hadn't had time to go up there much. But after Reagan declared the city an occupied zone, I knew the helicopters. Just outside on Saturday hanging clothes on the line, their whir and clatter, sudden, right overhead, giant insects. The cockpits like eyes of huge flies. I'd be pruning roses, and there they'd be. Swooped right down, cruised, hovered. You could see the guys' faces, sun glasses, looking.

Jeff would ring our door bell anytime, even at midnight. There he'd be on the front step, springing up and down on his legs, jerky, like a battery-operated toy not yet run down. First chair horn in the high school jazz band, he'd helped Greg out in the orchestra till he graduated. In the neighborhood, he'd say. Gotta take a leak. Wouldn't even shut the bathroom door. Strip off his T-shirt, soap his pits. We wouldn't always hear his bike roaring up the street. He'd park on the lawn. His old man was on his case all the time and he wasn't even dealing any more. We'd watch TV, Greg in the threadbare armchair, gallon of red half empty on the floor. Jeff would plop down on the paisley-covered mattress we used for a couch, sprawl out next to me. You got a fox here in the missus, he'd say to Greg while blowing smoke rings, but you know that, don'cha, a stone fox, right here, and he'd raise his bare arms to cradle his head, his cigarette the highest point of light in the room. The hair of his armpits was dark and fine. Good thing I know you're taking care of business, he'd say to Greg, and take another drag. The TV screen flickered. You two are better than parents to me, I mean that. He'd turn on his side, look me in the eyes, face maybe six inches from mine. His long legs. Don't know what I'd do without you, he'd say. And then he'd jump up, slam the front door, out of there, not even saying goodbye.

A crashing out of sleep. Jangling, glass breaking. Thuds, from downstairs. Somebody screaming. Lois. Three a.m.

The relief when she'd moved into the flat downstairs. Weekends, afternoons, the tea kettle. Evenings, typewriter keys, the little bell. Once in a while, an LP, Judy Collins, or Vivaldi. A librarian, she'd said, in Albany, but she wrote on the side, and one of her stories had come out in *Playboy*. When I'd walk down the drive that sloped past her window, I could see she'd repainted the orange and purple walls a pale cream.

Four a.m. by the time the police got there and we were drinking coffee with Polly and Ben next door. At least 6' 6" this guy was, Ben said, telling us blow by blow how he'd grabbed his granddad's pistol out of the drawer, pulled on his pajama bottoms and run down the drive, jumped into Lois's kitchen window through the broken place, landed flat on his feet, held out the gun, and found he was pointing it higher and higher at the dude holding Lois in a stranglehold. You just put that thing down, man, the guy said. But Ben wouldn't leave till he knew Lois was okay. She was bleeding, he said, from her head and her arm, and crying.

Lois told us afterward she'd had to move every few months to get away from him. She didn't want to have to move again. They hadn't been lovers for three years. But he always found her. She hadn't been able to work him into a story.

ASPARAGUS

Ty liked the tips. Especially on that new style of pizza with everything on it. I did too. One night when we made dinner, we steamed asparagus, and ended up throwing out the stalks. Tough, Ty said, stringy. At home I'd put the tips in a soufflé, and the next day, Greg would eat the leftover stalks. He said he preferred them. Closer to the ground, thicker. Ty didn't like to cook, would rather order out, or fill up on ice cream. I loved the feel of shining bowls, spoons. My new wire whisks spilled out of a ceramic pot like metal flowers. Greg would come in while I was beating egg whites and pat my bottom so it jiggled, crack jokes about my big butt, little tits. When you grew your own asparagus, you couldn't harvest the spears for at least a year. Greg had started spending most of the weekends digging in the garden, the dirt solid clay. When I'd go down to help, my shoes would get so heavy, so caked with mud, I could barely make it back to the house.

An hour after dinner at Barney's, people would start leaving the living room. As if something pulled them. Funny little half smiles. One or two at a time. After the first couple of evenings, Greg would go too. I'd stay with the wives left in the living room, talk about relatives, or movies or books, all of us perched on the half-dozen not-yet-refinished chairs. The people who'd left had grabbed their can of beer or glass of wine—or bourbon or Scotch, brandy or Cointreau—from the floor or the credenza. They had their clothes on when they came back out. I never went farther than the kitchen. Greg always told me, though, about the sizes and shapes of all the tits, whose he liked best, which nipples. Once, around two, as we were leaving, right by the coat rack near the front door, he grabbed Jeanette's through her caftan, rubbed them slowly around and around under his cupped hands, grinning, and she just stood there, grinning back.

CAKE

I always bought the applesauce cake they sold in the teachers' lunch-room. The ladies with the hairnets behind the metal folding window sold it for forty-five cents. Raisins, and lemony icing, the brown cake just a bit spicy. But I tried not to give in. I had to get rid of the little bulge you could see at the top of my thighs when I wore my shortest minis. One day Fred told me—in kind of a whisper—that my skirt was so short my cheeks, that was the word he used, showed, and I probably shouldn't wear that dress. But he smiled—they're delicious, he said. I knew I turned red, even though I'd heard he liked men. And I didn't wear that dress again. I did pick up the pace of my Royal Canadian Air Force exercises. Maybe it wasn't only the dress. Maybe my buns just hung too low. Julie had shown me a good exercise—you walked across the room on your bottom. Really worked those muscles.

We were still in bed, a half hour left before I had to go home, when I asked him outright. Did you ever—with Diane Eisenberg? Yeah, he said, the year before you came. Just one time. Yeah, it was good, but not that good. I thought it would be, you know, those huge boobs, but she wants it all done for her, she just kind of lay there. I don't think she thought I was great either. I asked her, and she said, oh, about a C+, and laughed. We're friendly, though, I like Diane. The kids do too. The administrators always give her what she asks for, she gets the best schedules. She talks so quiet, that nice soft voice, her little smile that looks kind of sad—even the worst kids calm down around her.

He still liked remembering those rich ladies in the tennis clubs down in places like San Jose, or back in Boulder. They knew they'd been missing it. Doctor husbands, lawyers, too busy and important. Those women appreciated every little thing he did. He'd give them an hour lesson for their money, and then spend the rest of the afternoon dipping into their honey pot. Some of them were good tennis players. Three or four, he said, still write letters. See that picture over there? That's from one of them, she painted it. She went back to college, got her degree, teaches second grade now in Palo Alto. We'd been talking about Diane's decision to join Synanon, give over her salary and her car. She was marrying the director. No possessions. No wedding presents. A small ceremony, nobody from outside. But that wasn't the worst. She'd confided to Ty that her fiancé barely touched her, couldn't even keep it up long enough to come. It was all right, she said, and laughed her sad little laugh. She'd had enough hard dicks to last a lifetime. She admired his principles. She'd get used to it.

No, I hadn't heard of it. Ty was telling me everybody was talking about it, this Friedan woman. He had to read it for his class at Cal. Maybe I should read it. Yeah, why didn't I read it, and then he wouldn't have to, and I could write his paper for him. Easy for me. I said I didn't mind. Okay. When I finished reading the whole book he wanted to know what I thought. I wasn't sure. But I didn't have a hard time writing his paper. I just said things the way he'd say them, organized it all into paragraphs, made sure everything was correct. Did I like the book? I didn't know. Maybe my mother had been like the women Friedan wrote about—the problem that had no name. I didn't really want to talk about it, as long as the paper was good enough for him to turn in. And tonight—if I could stay with him, not have to go home.

SHOWERING

He liked to shower two, three, even four times a day. He never jumped right out of bed after, but within a half hour he'd be under the spray, running his hands over his hair, scouring his chest, cleaning all of himself. I would lie a long time with that liquid bit of him still inside. I'd never met his family. His mama would like me, he said. But he'd never have kids, he told me plenty of times. Too much weight hanging on a man, teaching was enough for him. He'd come back to the bedroom rubbing the nap of the towel across his long back, sit down beside me, and talk, tell me again about his aunties back in Georgia, his cousins, his uncle, his sister. I'd never been to the South, never to Georgia. Didn't know what grew there. Pecan trees maybe. Peaches. The shapes and shades of the leaves, the sizes and patterns of the branches—the way the fruit ripened on them—I had only a vague idea.

BULLSHIT

You shouldn't listen to that bullshit, he said. I was lotioning my legs. All those guys are full of bullshit, they're just trying it out on you, see how far they can get. You shouldn't listen to me either. I pulled on my pantyhose, up to my waist. Is it bullshit, then, everything you've said to me? Ty looked down at the bed, top sheet mostly on the floor. No. But it was at the first. You shouldn't have listened. You should stay with your husband. I zipped up the back of my dress. He moved away from the jungle sheets, brown, yellow, black and white tigers, giraffes, panthers, and stood over me, his head bent down to my eyes. His index finger brushed my chin. I didn't expect to be feeling this way about you. Get it? I didn't expect. You just looked like some good pussy. You hear me? You should stay with your husband, have some nice white babies. I turned to the mirror, put in one earring. Tiny ivory flowers. Bullshit, I said. I put in the other earring and turned around. Tell me something. What do you mean when you ask if it's your pussy? His arms were around me, stroking me, and he rested his cheek on the top of my head. Fingered my left earring, swaying it back and forth. Stroked my cheek. You be here. That's what it means. Doesn't sound like bullshit, I said. Doesn't sound all that hard, either. His mouth was moving my name through my hair. I don't know, he said. I don't think you know how hard it could get.

Little, and gray. Unobtrusive, I could blend in. A shell curving around me above the wheel. Secondhand, one of my Danish friends had needed to sell it, fast. Hundreds just like it. Anonymous. Nearly invisible in fog, at least two or three parked on his block. I knew his old girlfriend Joanie, who'd moved with him from Colorado, drove a blue one. They'd had their own lives for a couple of years now, dated other people. Still helped each other with car troubles, rent agreements, things like that. Sometimes on the Nimitz I'd see one of them off to the side, all crumpled in. They didn't do so well at high speeds, weren't really built for distances.

ENCOUNTER GROUP

Ty faced me across the circle. My lip was trembling. Can't some white people understand, aren't some of them okay, I had asked. He almost sneered back, leaning toward Roberta Gibson's shoulder, tell her, Robbie, tell her, tell them what's happened to you, tell them how it's no better than it used to be. He was looking across the blank space of stained carpet in Martin Luther King Junior High's library with the smell of burned coffee in the air, looking straight at me. The stain at my feet began to separate from the carpet's threads. It was a face. It was a head with a huge Afro, it was a cloud. A storm. I fixed my eyes on it as Robbie's voice began, listing the things whites had said, had done. The stain began to take over my sight, blurred through tears, but I couldn't, not here, not here, let them fall.

That's how people usually are, Ty was saying, slipping a Miles Davis record from its sleeve. It's a common pattern. I'd been telling him just how furious I was. Why did he have to be so negative in our encounter group Saturday? And yes, I answered, when he asked, I had gone home and had a really good time with my husband. We even took a drive up the coast on Sunday. Fog never lifted, but we had a real nice lunch in a restaurant. And yes, I had liked being with my husband, he'd never do anything like that in a group.

He was standing next to me pouring 7 Up. All the tiny bubbles, countless, a quiet hissing as they burst. He took his glass over to the couch. You're following the classic expected behavior pattern, he said, that's what the psychologists call it. His glass on the table. Coltrane now on the LP. Drizzle outside, January. People in a triangle—one of their partners does something they don't like, the other one all of a sudden looks real good. The faint sibilance of the turntable's needle following the groove. And Miles, taking over.

Three dozen of them, Ty said. And he could have ordered more. So he went ahead and got one for himself. The English racing kind with the skinny tires. Nobody seemed to care, he just turned in the order. Didn't know if he felt right about it, but then he'd be taking the kids on field trips, that was the great thing about the alternative schools, you didn't have to worry about schedules, he could order a bus for a whole day, they could leave early, get up to Marin, bike around Muir Woods. Why not? Kids would learn biking, nature, how to follow a trail. And nobody'd miss $350 when they were spending twelve thousand on bikes and a hundred grand for the whole department. Yeah, it didn't feel right. But the money didn't really belong to anybody. Might as well use it for a good cause.

GREAT DANE

He was only taking care of Lady till Joanie found a bigger place. A brindle, taller than the tops of his thighs, and calm, happy padding around his carpet. He ran her every day. Was keeping a few things for Joanie for a while. A chair, some records, a couple of blouses in the closet, a leather coat. There was a framed photo of her on the dresser.

He liked to bring Lady along when we met in the hills. Lady never bothered us, just sniffed around under dry leaves until we put our clothes on again and were ready to start walking. Inside his house, Lady left us alone. Only when we sat on his low sofa to watch tennis on TV, or listen to an LP, did Lady back herself up and lean her full weight against our legs.

One Saturday, I was taking my VW to the service place he'd told me about on San Pablo, when all of a sudden Lady came bounding up. I turned away just in time, but before I slid into my front seat and closed the door, I managed a quick sideways look at Joanie—thinner than in the photo, sharper, less makeup, facing a mechanic bent over the car. Not as new as mine, and darker. But the same model.

SATURDAY ALL-DAY EXTENSION CLASS

I decided to take it with Margie. We needed the credits to qualify for teaching the gifted kids. It sounded fun, a day in Golden Gate Park. He was there greeting seventeen of us, brown lion beard and buffalo sandals. Pete, his name was, but today we should call him Rambling Man, because that's what we were going to do, learn to ramble, take it slow. Nobody ever saw what they saw, he boomed, but today we were going to look, really look at everything around us, see what we saw. The fog had cleared already, ten in the morning, and the leaves of the shrubs were gleaming. We started off, Pete in the lead. Almost right away he stopped. Here's a fallen leaf, he said. One leaf, something we trample with our shoes and don't even notice. Let's examine this leaf. Veins, bruises, see here? Now each one of you stop, stop right where you are and reach down and pick up something, anything, near your feet. Okay? Got it in your hand? Now look at it. Stare right into it. His voice had stopped booming. Margie and I were trying not to laugh, couldn't meet each other's eyes. He was thick as a redwood trunk. Now, he said. Find a place to sit down and draw what you're holding in your hand. We found a place we could sit together on the sloped grass in the sun. Margie's M.A. was from Cal. She'd wanted to go on for a Ph.D. but she and her husband decided he should get his first, in history of the Far East, so that's why she was teaching ninth grade. I began to draw. Pete was lying under a tree a few yards away, his eyes closed. The sun brightened even more and everything became very quiet. I'd found a clump of petals. A whole bloom fallen from the tree, petals still curved in close to each other, not yet decomposed.

IMPROV AT ASILOMAR

The sand cold under the seat of my Levi's with the fire hot on my nose and cheeks, everybody shadowy against the flames. All day in the workshop. Drama Skills for the English Class. Warm-ups, pantomime, role playing—new ways to build self-esteem, lead to positive behavior, increase awareness of physical expressions. Amazing how much we'd done in a day. We'd brought a couple of jugs of Cribari to the beach and were passing around a joint. On my right was the woman who'd worn a low-cut blouse all day and kept bending over in front of Barney—Angie, her name was, the one who'd pushed her way into his car, and then kept telling him all the way to the beach what a great workshop leader he was. Charisma. Now she was lying on her side and her sounds were slurred. Frank had just announced *The Atlantic* had taken his first poem. Angie was sort of wriggling on the sand. I sipped my wine. Barney and I were talking about one of the warm-ups, how to use it in class. And then Frank stood up. Time to perform a public service, he said to nobody in particular, and walked over to Angie. The two of them moved a couple of yards off down the beach, away from the light of the fire. I could see him unbuckle his pants before they lay down. Everybody kept on talking. When Barney rolled another joint, I took a long drag before handing it back. We didn't start giggling until later.

PORTER

I was crying again. Loved him. Didn't he love me too. Why couldn't we get married. I wanted a baby with him. I reached for more Kleenex. Said through the sobs I just wanted him to love me like I loved him. I don't think you know what you really want, he said. And you don't act real lovable right now. But he kissed my neck, and held me for a while. You know I told you I couldn't do marriage, he said. Not this man. Not me. No way. Couldn't do it. But I'm here now, aren't I? I was calming down. Wiped my nose. Wadded the Kleenex into a hard wet ball.

Later that afternoon he told me about his first job on the trains. How much he liked it, especially the first class sleepers. Lots of ladies on those trains. The first time it happened he answered the bell the way he always did, knocked on the door of the compartment. There was this naked white lady on top of the bed with her legs all spread out, just there for him. Some of those ladies were rich, gave him presents sometimes. Most of them were real lonely. Rode his car a couple of times a month, made sure they knew his schedule.

Telling him what I'd give up for him. It wouldn't work, he said. I was frying the bacon, he was stirring eggs. Instant coffee, Tang. He'd bought a kitchen table, big enough for two people to sit down to a meal. Green formica, matching chairs. The fog had lifted, a peek-through view of the bay from the window over the sink. He didn't want to live with somebody all the time. I wanted to zip open his chest and climb inside. But didn't I realize, he was saying, dropping the bread in the toaster, I wouldn't like it. He'd always be playing tennis, or basketball with the coaches. Yeah he liked movies, and sure we liked to talk about people and the kids and school and even books sometimes, but I'd get frustrated, he knew I would, and I needed to accept that. And besides, he'd told me over and over, no marriage for him, no big commitments. Enough of this kind of talk, let's eat breakfast, he said, and we did, watching the sunlight play on the rose bushes outside. After the dishes, he stroked my hair before he helped me get ready to go.

HATCHED

I liked Ty's place better, mine had too many windows to the street, too easy to see in. I liked driving over to his place, parking, waiting a few minutes to make sure no one I knew was going by, and then striding out, as if I belonged there, to the sidewalk leading up to his door. And his opening it, his little smile. The brush past his tall body to go on in—or, the door closing and the two of us staying put, my purse dropping to the floor. At his place, he took care of things. Only his mail, dishes, his laundry.

But Greg was still away and my zebra finches' eggs had hatched. Embarrassed for Ty to come so close to the mess of the cage—newsprint at the bottom musty with droppings, scattered with millet—but I wanted him to see. I led him to the back room, to the big cage on the far wall, and pointed him to the round opening of the wooden box hanging inside. Tiny, the hatchlings, littler than your thumbnail. Scrawny, bald, their swollen and still-blind eyes. Dark inside the dark enclosure. He peered his head around the door. But he couldn't make them out.

BALLOONS

Even with Greg out of town, I worried. The neighbors might see. And Ty wasn't exactly an invisible man. Not that the neighborhood was all white, but his height, his baldness, his black and tan Mustang. I wasn't saying no, I just wasn't sure I wanted to right now. Wasn't sure. I was staring at my left knee, my legs crossed over the carpet. I just didn't feel safe anymore. So much strong feeling and no public place to smile it, sing it, shine it out. Like that musical we'd seen together, *Black Balloons*, the hundreds of balloons let loose in the theater and floating, floating higher and higher as if all our heads, hair, all those naturals were lifting, lifted up over the heavy rows of hard wooden chairs. And everybody carrying balloons, airy, shining, out into the San Francisco streets before they popped.

BASEMENT

The way to the garden behind the house. Damp smell of old things. Once Greg had found a World War Two shell case among the piled up *Reader's Digests,* *Saturday Evening Posts,* and *National Geographics.* I used it for a vase. That second summer Greg was away working on his doctorate, Ty brought over some stuff to store down there while he was closing on his house. Wool sweaters, cotton sweatshirts, Converse shoes, LP's. Cardboard losing its stiffness in the damp. His jackets, jeans, draped over the blades of Greg's tools, the base of the electric drill, the old metal trunk with the sharp corners. He'd hung on to a couple of sweaters, a windbreaker. July could be foggy, chilly. Especially on the coast, and we wanted to take a little trip or two the way we had last year. Always cold by the ocean, no matter how warm the sand felt. One Saturday Greg surprised me by driving home for the weekend. He'd missed me, he told me in the kitchen. And a whole month left before he could come home, start the new school year. He didn't even bring his dirty laundry, never once went near the door to the stairs leading the way down.

COLD

Ty didn't think I needed to spend so much time on how I looked. But I sure did look good, he said, in that new blue soft dress. And what was this talk about my not driving over to his house afternoons. Nobody'd found out, had they. What was he going to do if I didn't come over and give him some at least sometimes. Maybe not the way we'd been doing, maybe only once a week. Or twice, twice'd be good. Why'd I have to be talking like this right now, when I knew he was thinking about cutting out ice cream because of his new little pot belly. Cramp his style if he had a big old belly hanging out. I knew he'd just decided to cut down to single scoops. And he knew I could handle two men, I'd been doing it all this time. He could see if maybe I'd decided to put the lid back on the honey pot once in a while. But to take it away— cold. He walked across the room to me. His chin dropped down to my forehead. Nuzzling. A whisper. Could I say no to this.

GIMME FIVE

Julie was always low-fiving somebody. With the principal, the coaches, the head counselor, even Willie Jones when he told her he hadn't missed one class in the last six weeks, no blue slip sent home to his mother this time. Anybody male, she held out her palm, her bright red nails facing the floor, and said *gimme five,* her San Francisco private girls' school speech dropping east, down, and south by half a dozen states. Even in a miniskirt, she did the lean forward, the dip down from the hips with the back straight and almost horizontal to the ground, one knee lifted up toward the chin, and finally, the laugh. I could never get it right. But you didn't see the other women teachers doing it, especially not the black women. And you never saw them in miniskirts. True, the girls' track coach Louise walked around in her gym suit all the time, but you never saw Ardis Baine or Roberta Gibson, with her groomed little Afro, in a skirt much above their knees. Julie was almost one of the guys—talked football, basketball, passes, tight ends, overtime with all of them. Only a few people knew about her mother, so bad an alcoholic she couldn't even look up to focus on whoever came through the door, let alone put an arm around her daughter's shoulder. Been that way off and on for years. And her father—I met him once at their clothing store. He gave me a discount. But I heard him complaining to Julie, he wished his daughter could help him out sometimes on the floor. He was sure she had some spare time once in a while, she didn't have to teach on weekends did she, couldn't she give him a few hours once a week or so?

INVITATION

Hand-written, on a card with roses on the cover and a gold script *Thank You*. Come for coffee, after school, next Thursday. Frances had been telling me for weeks her mother wanted to meet me. Could I come, please. She liked to stay after class, help straighten desks. Sometimes she'd come into my room over lunch and write in her journal, her tidy writing. She said she'd never raised her hand in class before this year. Her mother shook my hand hard, brought her other hand up over mine. I can't thank you enough for what you've done for this young lady, she said. Frances never had faith in herself till she was in your class. Doilies on the chairs, perked coffee in thin cups with saucers, cookies and slices of spice cake. Sun through white curtains. Frances swept her pleated skirt under her as she sat down. Her mother asked where I was from, how long I'd been married. I hate to see a good teacher like you quit, she said, handing me a refilled cup of coffee, but you're going to want babies, aren't you, same as I did. I don't know what I'd do without my Frances. My comfort and my joy. You need some babies, honey, she said again. Don't let those people at that school mess with you, don't let them mess with your head, you hear what I'm saying? You got your own life, your husband, don't you? I hear from Frances, how you be there for the kids, how some of them call you in your own home. She bit into a cookie. You can't be giving yourself to other people's kids all the time, she said. You need to save some of yourself for your own.

ORGANIC

Greg brought home a five-gallon stainless steel pot from a store he'd found in *The Whole Earth Catalog*. For canning things. And he'd picked up a case of glass jars, metal lids, and the rings that screwed down over them. Peaches, apricots. Boil them up. He found a recipe in the *Chronicle* for brandied cherries. Got out the copy of *Mastering the Art of French Cooking* that my mother had given us for our anniversary. *Boeuf bourguignon*. A slow simmer. Hardly any bubbles, you had to keep the heat down low, use plenty of wine. And maybe it was time for a family. His pile of compost was already feeding the tomatoes. The new books that had come in the mail from Rodale Press explained how we could be a self-sufficient unit, grow all our own food, even wheat, grind it ourselves, raise chickens for protein. The secret was compost. We could recycle our scraps.

ANSWERING MACHINE

We got one because Helen Cornwell wouldn't stop calling. Middle
of the night, how this time she'd really do it. I'd pick up the phone
breathless from running down the hall. Silence. Little gasps through
the receiver and then, the slow intake of a breath, and sputtering. At
school Helen would slink down the edge of the hall. Thick and slow,
frizzy pale red hair around her slumped shoulders. Vague-eyed, till
she spotted me. Her left hand had begun speaking to her in a language
she was beginning to understand. Her right hand was interfering. She
might cut it off. She was only safe in my classroom. She had written
thirty new pages in her journal. I was the only one who understood.
Couldn't I talk with her after school again, meet her somewhere. She
dreamed I was her Angel, her Bright Savior. Little gifts appeared on
my desk. A braided bookmark. A candle. At first the calls came in the
evenings. Then after two weeks of being waked at three in the morn-
ing, I told Julie. The answering machine was her idea, she knew where
to get one. Helen quit calling. But Julie was practically the only one
who left a message. Relatives, friends—they just hung up.

BLOODSTONE

Over and over the same families of words. Lester was trying. Side by side in the brown chairs at the table. Battle, tattle, rattle, brother, another, click, flick, nick, fight, tight, night. Luck—no, keep him on track. Let's do some writing, I said. Head almost touching the table, he gripped the pen, pressed down hard. His small motions, impatience, there, that good enough? So, some reading. A story. Somebody doing something. On the street. Till I took my eyes off the page and saw my ring sliding off my finger. No. No, Lester. I had his attention. You like this ring? he asked. Yes, I like it, I said. But you couldn't get much for it. Please don't try that again. See, it belonged to my granny's mother in England, where my mother's from. I've never been there. A blood-stone, the green was almost black, the red veins and pools so tiny that, until now, they had been almost invisible.

OIL SPILL

Karen talked me into going over that night, said they'd been working around the clock, they needed everybody they could get. Thousands of birds. Cages. Mostly grebes. Feathers clotted in thick crude oil so they couldn't fly. The warehouse a hive, a make-do hospital, everybody working in twos and threes—pony tails, headbands, long sweeps of straight hair fanning down over pairs of hands. One to press the wings—with the thumbs—close to the body, keep the bones of the wings from spreading out, and, with the fingers, hold the cold webbed feet immobile. Another to hold the beak shut, everyone had been bitten. One moment of relaxing the pressure and—panic, flapping, out of control. Hundreds of lean backs bent together in small groups over birds, swabbing with detergent. The grebes' red eyes. No one knew the detergent removed the birds' natural oils. Nobody knew that when the birds were released, their feathers would absorb the water they had always surfaced on, to rest. It wouldn't take long for them to drown.

LAST

If it meant going dead I would rather. Better just not see him, or talk. I can't even come in and sit in one of the kid's desks next to you at lunch time? he said. Not even that. If the soil were packed down hard, solid clay like the earth around the old mildewed roses, no room for air, no sand or humus, maybe nothing more would grow through. Tamp it all down, not even room for a strand. The answer was no. Take the green pillow case I had kept and fold it into a box and seal it with tape. Same box for the photo of his big head in front of a redwood, smiling at me. Put it all away. Close down shop. Move back to the desert.

ALWAYS

In winter the rain. I was remembering Hemingway, wanting to teach *A Farewell.* Mr. Hewitt said he didn't think these kids were too young, whatever I thought would be relevant. I remembered how in the novel Catherine said she saw herself dead in it. January so damp and chilly my shoulders tensed from hunching under my umbrella. I didn't care whether it was good for the students. I wanted to reread Hemingway. And *The Sun Also Rises.* How they tried to learn to live after that war. I wanted to find the part in *Farewell* about the dog, toward the end, nosing the garbage cans. *There isn't anything, dog*—that line. Some of the kids didn't get it that the baby was already dead—or maybe they just didn't finish.

EMPTY LOT

Turning another corner onto the lot thigh-high with anise flowering. Pungent, airy yellow, a vague scent of childhood. Almost a vertical slope, barely room for a foothold down into the property. So overgrown you couldn't see the bay.

We'd often walked there, summertime, afternoons. Sometimes we tried to imagine building. Slippery. We found the one place we could sit side by side, without fearing we might slide. Where I told him.

A complete severance. Long after I had moved away, I found myself walking there during a visit back to see friends. The anise gone to seed. No one had been able to build on that steepness.

TOOLS

I gave them all away. Frames, dowels, the hand-rubbed comb Ruth had given me. The sword. Even the yarns. Spools, coils, wound balls— boxes and baskets of textures, metallic, thin, angora, nubby, dozens of shades of colors. I'd had an idea for a tapestry. Two huge trees, the whole thing would be seven feet high. Partly woven, partly stitched. I wasn't sure how I'd do it. The bark would be mottled. Each tree different, one birch-like, silvery, maybe a eucalyptus, and the other like a pine, or redwood, darker, taller. But the leaves would intermingle, you would hardly be able to tell which tree they came from. I'd have needed an eight harness loom. Would do the roots first. Reaching, lacing, interlocking, a base for the design, threads that would have followed.

DESSERTS

The year after I left him, I got into French cooking. Desserts. Best was the Charlotte Malakoff. Ladyfingers. Squeezed from the cloth bag with the silvery nipple. Fragile in their rising on the pan, flaky tongues, sifted over with powdered sugar. Whitest white, creamy white. Pale fingers upright in the mold, holding the dark mousse inside. The bitter chocolate and heavy cream, pulverized almonds, sugar beaten in butter, and a liqueur that cost so much we'd be down to the wire halfway to payday. The first time I made it, our friends around the table stood up and applauded. All the hands clapping, hands slapping against their own. Mine lay in my lap. But after they'd gone and my husband was sleeping, I'd run my fingers across the plate, scraping what was left.

MINISKIRTS

How short was short? Trying them on at Julie's mom and dad's dress shop in the Marina, I wanted them as high as I could get but not show the bottom curve of my buns. At least when I was standing up.

That was three years before Julie killed herself, Julie who knew without question her boobs were her best attribute, who wouldn't lose weight, carried a little extra because if she dropped even a couple of pounds, they shrank. One of the PE teachers, which one was it, said Julie had a big sloppy pussy, really liked to be gone down on, but in the end, after she'd been found dead with the principal's baby inside her—someone said he'd refused to divorce his wife in Oakland, and Julie had wanted to get married and have his baby no matter how black—in the end, it turned out it was the girls' track coach, Louise, who'd wanted her most, and Julie couldn't decide. By then I was long gone. Earth shoes, corduroys, no makeup. Hell with it. Just do what you gotta do, get on with it.

AFTER

Color, even in rain. Tie-dye, paisley, fringes. Afros, naturals. His hovering at my classroom door, racket brushing his leg. A blanket in the hills under the redwoods, the eucalyptus, their brown seeds like bells. After school. His bedspread the colors of moss, of leaves. And month after month, on his sheets with the brown stripes, furrows across his bed, we laid our two selves down, while around us on the streets, in the parks, the halls of the ninth-grade school we taught in, the students swirled like uprooted flowers, seeds with no good dirt to drop down into. He asked me to write his graduate papers for him (and I did), and he always asked (and I always answered yes), if it was still his pussy. Summers, my husband gone, we'd spend nights, go out for ice cream late. 31 Flavors. Double cones rose from our hands, so many, so many possible combinations.

ACKNOWLEDGMENTS

Many thanks to the editors of the magazines in which some of these prose poems or flash fiction pieces first appeared: *The Antioch Review,* for "Tennis"; *The Chariton Review,* for "Cross Weave" and "Stitchery"; *Confrontation,* for "Friday Night With the English Teachers" and "On the Bay"; *Folio,* for "Eggplant"; *The Laurel Review,* for "Shop Talk," "Slipping In," and *"Kind of Blue"*; *Mississippi Review,* for "Teachers' Lounge" and "Invitation"; *New York Quarterly,* for "Freed Up"; and *Ontario Review,* for "After School," "Audio Visual," "Bullshit," "Half and Half," "Oil Spill," "Remedial Reading," "Teaching *Uncle Tom's Children,"* and "What You Got." "Improv at Asilomar" appeared in *Suddenly: An Anthology of Sudden Fiction and Prose Poetry, III;* "Gimme Five" and "Macramé" appeared in *Suddenly: An Anthology of Sudden Fiction and Prose Poetry, IV.*

I am grateful to the University of Texas at San Antonio for a writing leave and to the Rockefeller Foundation for a Residency Fellowship at the Villa Serbelloni in Bellagio.

Heartfelt thanks to my graduate students, and to Sharon Ankrum, Vera Banner, Laurence Barker, Kevin Clark, David Dooley, Cyra Dumitru, Jennifer Gates, Sandra M. Gilbert, Sue Hum, Paulette Jiles, Catherine Kasper, Jeannine Keenan, Steven G. Kellman, Sonja Lanehart, Doran Larson, David Dodd Lee, Christine Dumaine Lesche, Robert Lescher, Bonnie Lyons, Patricia McConnell, Sherry McKinney, Alicia Ostriker, Barbara Ras, Heather Sellers, Melissa Shepherd, Amritjit Singh, Veda Smith, Barbara Stanush, Hannah Stein, and David Ray Vance. I'm very grateful to Martha Rhodes, Michael Neff at Del Sol Press, and Ander Monson. And to Pierre Crosson, who, at Bellagio, insisted I begin.

WENDY BARKER's previous collections include *Poems from Paradise, Way of Whiteness, Let the Ice Speak,* and *Winter Chickens.* She has also published three chapbooks. *Poems' Progress* includes a selection of poems accompanied by personal essays, and her translations (with Saranindranath Tagore), *Rabindranath Tagore: Final Poems,* received the Sourette Diehl Fraser Award from the Texas Institute of Letters. Her poems have appeared in many journals and magazines, including *The American Scholar, Boulevard, Georgia Review, Gettysburg Review, Poetry, Southern Review,* and *Southwest Review.* Recipient of NEA and Rockefeller fellowships, she is also the author of *Lunacy of Light: Emily Dickinson and the Experience of Metaphor,* and co-editor (with Sandra M. Gilbert) of *The House is Made of Poetry: The Art of Ruth Stone.* She is Poet-in-Residence and a professor of English at the University of Texas at San Antonio.

DEL SOL PRESS, based out of Washington, D.C., publishes exemplary and edgy fiction, poetry, and nonfiction (mostly contemporary, with the occasional reprint). Founded in 2002, the press sponsors two annual competitions:

THE DEL SOL PRESS POETRY PRIZE is a yearly booklength competition with a January deadline for an unpublished book of poems.

THE ROBERT OLEN BUTLER PRIZE is awarded for the best short story, published or unpublished. The deadline is in November of each year.

HTTP://WEBDELSOL.COM/DSP

CPSIA information can be obtained at www.ICGtesting.com
Printed in the USA
LVOW131728210812

295315LV00006B/83/P